THE NIGHT SHIFT

Edited by
Michael Baron,
Andy Croft and Jenny Swann

Foreword by
John Humphrys

Five Leaves Publications

www.fiveleaves.co.uk

THE NIGHT SHIFT

Edited by Michael Baron,
Andy Croft and Jenny Swann

Published in 2010
by Five Leaves Publications,
PO Box 8786, Nottingham NG1 9AW
www.fiveleaves.co.uk

ISBN: 978 1 905512 58 4

Five Leaves acknowledges financial support
from Arts Council England

Five Leaves is represented by Turnaround,
distributed to the trade by Central Books
and is a member of Inpress
(www.inpressbooks.co.uk)

Design and typeset by
Four Sheets Design and Print

Printed in Great Britain

CONTENTS

THE CRUMPLED DUVET

ACKNOWLEDGEMENTS

FOREWORD

John Humphrys

There are two questions *Today* presenters are asked with infuriating regularity. One of them is: "Do the politicians know the questions beforehand?" The answer is no. How could they when even I don't know what questions I will ask until I ask them? The questions depend on the answers.

The other is: "What time do you have to get up in the morning?" and the answer is: "We don't". We get up in the middle of the night. We crawl from our pits when normal, sane, untroubled souls are settling into their deepest sleep and when the body and soul are at their most vulnerable. This is when, as nurses will tell you, sick people on the edge of death finally slip away into whatever awaits them in the next world. These are the bleakest hours. The soft, apologetic light of dusk has long since faded and dawn is not yet even a promise.

Or so I viewed it when, as a relatively young man more than twenty years ago, I began the *Today* routine. The first time the alarm rang at 3.30a.m. on a January morning I tried to pretend that it was all a silly joke. I hadn't really been serious when I had said I would give up my cosy billet as a television newsreader ... had I?

God, it was hellish in those early days. And now? Well, it's still hellish – of course it is – but there are compensations. There is the "beauty of the morning" to be found even in the mean streets of west London. They may not be quite as "silent, bare" as they were when Wordsworth wrote *Composed Upon Westminster Bridge* two centuries ago. The great man might have been shocked at the last, loud drunks staggering across roads, shivering girls teetering on high heels in their wake, avoided by weary taxi drivers. Or possibly not.

This is a different place from how it will be in three hours' time when the traffic will clog every inch of these empty roads. You feel a touch of envy for those still in their warm, sleeping houses – but also a touch of superiority. In a few hours you will be going home – job done, politicians skewered or not, audience satisfied or cross – and everyone else will be going to work.

I have no idea of the statistics, but most poets who choose to write about the night seem to find their inspiration in town rather than country: the "starless and bible-black" town of Dylan Thomas; the *Night Waitress* of Lynda Hull "bitter with sleeplessness"; God speaking to Vernon Scannell "beyond the dark sky and its white rash of stars on a frosty night on Ealing Broadway".

But I have had another (almost) night job: milking cows on a farm in west Wales. There is real beauty in the wintry pre-dawn hour of a farm: the cows' breath and sweat mingling in misty patches; the frost fringing trees and grass and the silence before the dogs wake and the work begins.

One day, when *Today* is a memory, I shall write about it. But there's enough in this delightful anthology to last until then.

INTRODUCTION

This anthology celebrates the romance of the awake world at night and also draws attention to its more shady and brutal side. The poems are in three themed sections; the first, 'A Hard Day's Night', focuses on paid workers who ply their trade at night; the second, 'In the Forests of the Night' describes the animal kingdom, the world of nature, active under cover of darkness. The third, 'A Crumpled Duvet', pans across all those who are alive to the highs and lows of being awake at night – with insomnia, sleepless babies or late night revelry.

A HARD DAY'S NIGHT

When Michael Palin first sang, 'I'm a lumberjack and I'm OK, I sleep all night and I work all day' he was stating the bleedin' obvious. In Britain in the late 1960s the great majority of people worked during the day and slept at night.

Today, however, an estimated seven million Britons are described as being 'economically active at night'. The dramatic expansion of the 24-hour economy means that this figure is unlikely to decrease. In developed economies almost one fifth of the working population now works at night. Working at night is bad for your health. It is not for nothing that night work is sometimes called the graveyard shift. It disrupts the circadian rhythm, the body's biological clock.

Night shift workers work longer shifts than day workers. They are statistically more likely to be involved in car accidents on the way home from work. They are easily exploited and easy to blame when things go wrong (the disasters at Three Mile Island, Chernobyl, Bhopal and Exxon Valdez have all been blamed on night shift workers).

Socialists have historically been opposed to night shift work as exploitative and dehumanising. The Paris Commune prohibited the production of bread at night ('the workers should educate themselves, but how can you educate yourself when you work at night?'). For the same reasons, in 1917 the Bolsheviks prohibited all work between 8pm and 6am.

And yet who has not envied the nightshift workers clocking-off just as you arrive for work? Which one of us has not felt a guilty and grateful fascination for those who work at night in our hospitals, airports and emergency services?

We know that without the nocturnal labours of cleaners, porters, truckers, bouncers, cabbies, bakers, bar staff, train-drivers, printers and milkmen the daylight world could not function. And yet night shift workers are invisible. They are the Morlocks of the modern world, living below-stairs, the painting in the attic, our guilty conscience, the walking wounded, the undead. And they are of course all too often invisible in contemporary British literature.

W.H. Auden's "Night Mail" – written for the GPO Film Unit – reminds us that British culture was not always so incurious about its economic foundations. Auden was writing in a period which also produced James Curtis's *They Drive by Night* (1938), Inez Holden's novel about women in a war-time munitions factory *Night Shift* (1941), Paul Rotha's *Night Shift* (1942) and J.B. Priestley's *Daylight on Saturday* (1944).

Almost half of the poems in the first section of the anthology come from the USA, where the world of work – especially casual, low-paid, manual work – is still central to myths of selfhood and nationhood. There is a strong culture of blue-collar poetry in the USA (there are for example, several US websites dedicated solely to poetry by long-distance truckers). They even celebrate National Nightshift Workers' Day.

This section asserts the ordinariness of night shift work, its dull rituals and comfortable routines, its winners and losers. The poems record the exhaustion and boredom, the bleak and painful weirdness of working while the world is asleep. They include those who – like taxi-drivers, waitresses, bouncers, musicians, gamblers, prostitutes and drug-dealers – inhabit the twilight world between work and pleasure, legality and crime, night and day. And they address the loneliness of the night shift, 'the men who never see their wives', who 'think of home and the wife who sleeps alone in the bed that a truck bought', returning each morning 'to beds warmed by/impressions of wives'.

Let us now praise the night shift. Perhaps it is time we had a National Nightshift Workers' Day – or Night? – in the UK. (AC)

IN THE FORESTS OF THE NIGHT

At night, in forest, field, garden, house, in watery places, poets have strange meetings, unexpected collisions and collusions with animals.

9

Not every poet sleeps his or her full ration. Ted Hughes once wrote of being awake and at work on a blank page "... I see no stars..." but he knew the deepening darkness conceals the fox about to enter the dark hole of the head. Thomas Hardy one August midnight records how the room is full of insects, including "a sleepy fly" that will smudge his "new-penned line", undoing his good work.

Far from Wessex, and a century later, Paul Muldoon and his dog, Angus, eye up a coyote while Anne Stevenson out with her dog among streetlights and shadows is not a lone walker but 'three of us'.

Gilbert White of Selbourne is curious as he wanders through a fairy landscape as it sinks into night, and finds solace in its "soothing melancholy joy". Also taking comfort from the night, in which "The heart is asleep, and in the heart, anxiety" is Radnóti who, in the last few months of his life (he will be executed by firing squad on a November night) finds peace in a Hungarian garden.

The poems are filled with skies unpolluted by city lights but whirring with wings – Graham Mort's Ugandan sky is awake with bats and storm and heat, while John Keats sits in his Hampstead garden and spins an exquisite poem out of the song of a nightingale.

Meanwhile Edward Thomas spares a thought for all those who have to sleep out of doors on a cold night.

Under cover of dark, animals have reason to fear not just each other but the activities of people too. Neil Rollinson's father is out breaking ice to drown four kittens. Elsewhere, Tom Rawling is night fishing.

Yet all is not death and destruction; love has not gone, not for deer, toads and the elusive natterjack, as Jane Routh and Jean Sprackland testify.

The natural world at night is a secret place, an expanse of mystery in which these poems shine their small torches, uncovering creatures awake in darkness that depend on each other or avoid each other, for survival.

(MB)

THE CRUMPLED DUVET

In addition to those people working the night shift and nocturnal creatures busy trying to enact their killing work or to avoid being killed under cover of darkness, who else is awake at night for one reason or another?

Lovers, parents with sleepless babies, party-goers teetering home, travellers, the joyous, the gloomy, the sociable, and the solitary – poems form themselves as the night wears on and the world sleeps.

Evening finds Frances Cornford celebrating the magical changeover from day to night while Vernon Scannell – by his own confession, the worse for drink – experiences a numinous moment on Ealing Broadway.

Elaine Feinstein lies in bed thinking about life and death and the strange yet reassuring human habit of prayer. Mark Haworth-Booth's couple hear their neighbours return home in the dark, their violent taunts and rowing. Meanwhile Mark Murphy's "Night-Watch: Man and Muse" surveys a sleeping town "groaning under the weight of its own contradictions" in which, at night, the only comfort that will do, is "the stranger's voice on the phone".

In another town, "moonless... starless and bible-black", Dylan Thomas' imagination pans out across the darkness, listening in on the dreams of sleepers.

Among the hundreds of candidates jostling for a place as the ultimate night-time sex scene, Don Juan gets the job... but we are left with enough material to bring out a whole new anthology of erotic poems set at night. Maybe another time.

Come midnight, and Samuel Taylor Coleridge sits in front of a dying fire deep in the winter countryside. Everyone else has gone to bed "save that at my side/ My cradled infant slumbers peacefully".

By 3a.m. Steven Blyth is up with his baby son, administering the night feed while Eavan Boland tiptoes into her daughter's room as dawn breaks, to lift her up, "Wriggling/In your rosy, zipped sleeper".

4a.m. sees Maura Dooley driving through the darkness, alone with the car radio. The moon lights the way for Walter de la Mare's traveller to his ghost-thronged house in the forest; it shines out over the sea as Matthew Arnold watches from his window.

By 5a.m. Fleur Adcock speaks for us all as she lies awake in bed remembering the humiliations and suspicions and betrayals that are the stuff of daily life but that come to "stand icily about the bed looking worse and worse/and worse" in the small hours.

As dawn breaks, William Wordsworth crosses London, and, looking out of his coach window, comes up with the definitive sonnet describing the view of an early morning London in which "the very houses seem asleep". More than two hundred years later, W. S. Graham wanders round the mythology of London at night, ending up "like a flea crouched/In the stopped works of a watch".

As the night ends, Simon Armitage and his partner, who are working different shifts, keep missing each other by minutes, the duvet still warm on the bed the other has only recently risen from, communication via "lipstick love-notes on the bathroom mirror".

Elsewhere, Tennyson stands grieving inconsolably outside the dark house of his dead friend as "On the bald street breaks the blank day".

Another night is over, rich in its discoveries, poignant in its loneliness. The lovers' bowers lie empty, the moon has thinned to a ghost, and the day girds up its loins, ready to swing into action as the night shift workers make their tired way home. (JS)

A HARD
DAY'S NIGHT

NIGHT MAIL
(Commentary for a GPO Film)

W.H. Auden

I

This is the Night Mail crossing the Border,
Bringing the cheque and the postal order,

Letters for the rich, letters for the poor,
The shop at the corner, the girl next door.

Pulling up Beattock, a steady climb:
The gradient's against her, but she's on time.

Past cotton-grass and moorland boulder,
Shovelling white steam over her shoulder,

Snorting noisily, she passes
Silent miles of wind-bent grasses.

Birds turn their heads as she approaches,
Stare from bushes at her blank-faced coaches.

Sheep-dogs cannot turn her course;
They slumber on with paws across.

In the farm she passes no one wakes,
But a jug in a bedroom gently shakes.

II

Dawn freshens. Her climb is done.
Down towards Glasgow she descends,
Towards the steam tugs yelping down a glade of cranes,
Towards the fields of apparatus, the furnaces
Set on the dark plain like gigantic chessmen.
All Scotland waits for her:
In dark glens, beside pale-green lochs,
Men long for news.

III

Letters of thanks, letters from banks,
Letters of joy from girl and boy,
Receipted bills and invitations
To inspect new stock or to visit relations,
And applications for situations,
And timid lovers' declarations,
And gossip, gossip from all the nations,
News circumstantial, news financial,
Letters with holiday snaps to enlarge in,
Letters with faces scrawled on the margin,
Letters from uncles, cousins and aunts,
Letters to Scotland from the South of France,
Letters of condolence to Highlands and Lowlands,
Written on paper of every hue,
The pink, the violet, the white and the blue,
The chatty, the catty, the boring, the adoring,
The cold and official and the heart's outpouring,
Clever, stupid, short and long,
The typed and the printed and the spelt all wrong.

IV

Thousands are still asleep,
Dreaming of terrifying monsters
Or a friendly tea beside the band in Cranston's or
    Crawford's:
Asleep in working Glasgow, asleep in well-set
    Edinburgh,
Asleep in granite Aberdeen,
They continue their dreams,
But shall wake soon and hope for letters,
And none will hear the postman's knock
Without a quickening of the heart.
For who can bear to feel himself forgotten?

NOSFERATU

Bob Beagrie

After the Winter weakened sun has set
Behind bloated cooling towers that form a net
With gantries, chimneys, rusting cranes
As if to catch, to hoard stray flames
Dripping like spills of Lindisfarne mead
Down frozen girders of a darkened screed.

This is when we take our turn
To stalk the world in plain nocturne
To ride the thirst, to hunt, to feed
Between neon lights of lust and greed
Most mortal lives that pack these streets
Believe themselves to be gods, not sheep.

Not the branded livestock of a battery farm
Bred to break, for culling, to domesticate
To turn on each other as we watch and wait.
Like that gang of lads, huddled, chipping in
For a tenner wrap of old Mickey Finn, who sells
The very finest smack, uncut Charlie, Billy Wizz

From around the back and through a grill
As fairy lights flash across his window sill.
Live it up mortal children. Party. Shop. Copulate.
Blinkered to the touch of your stone cold fate,
Like those dozy burglars who take the piss
Who'd nick the hope of a Christmas kiss

From the new lass among the admin staff
At the sparkling clad Karaoke bash, like the
Teenage girl arguing on her mobile phone
Under a billboard poster for Toblerone,
Keeping an eye, a nod an ass cheek on
The pan of headlights for Mercs and Jags.

And shivering she sparks another
Marlborough fag, posing for punters,
Johns and pimps, human vampires,
King prawns and shrimps; the small fry
Gangsters of a Northern town bleeding
Little Cinders in her skin tight gown.

All the while Nosferatu watch and wait
Select our meals from this rich palate.
So watch your back if you venture out,
We blend in well with the average lager lout
And step with care so as not to skid
On the icy roads of this urban grid.
And thank the daylight when it returns
For all those we've kissed will fear its burn.

TOO LATE

Alison Brackenbury

There is a dark and hungry hour
before this bed
when nothing is awake
but owls, hedgehogs, bats and deer,
drivers and nurses watch their dials flicker;
lovers; the yawning engineer
patient as porridge, after storms have torn
through power-lines, must twist and test each wire,
till pylons heave and crackle
before dawn.

ODE TO THE NIGHT SHIFT FREIGHT WORKER

Erin E. Elder

The world doesn't know who stands outside on a
    summer night
Peering at the handbill as a cloud passes over the moon.
Suicide bomber moths crash into the glare of his
    flashlight
He will brush them way and grimly load.

Wheels roaring in the distance, rattle and clang as they
    near
A familiar face leans out of a half opened truck window
And waves a friendly hand. Loneliness is interrupted for
    a few hours.
Though no one has time to speak or to visit more than a
    quip or a sneer.

The gnats are maddening. They know it and rejoice.
Partaking in the sweat that travels from forehead to
    contact lens
They multiply and swarm every day until it gets cold.
Not too soon they are replaced with flocks of birds
    and leaves

Flocks of birds and leaves are replaced by nothing...
    only cold.
Soul-chilling, bone-hurting, eye stinging cold.
Dry and wet cold alternate. The workers long for July,
    forgetting past insects
And remembering children who will find holiday things
    because they work outside.

They work outside in the wind with tight-lipped smiles
    to keep their teeth from freezing.

The driver returns and brings something this time. He
   grins as he opens his door
And steps down with something to share that might
   warm them up.
After a few jokes and bites of parking lot pizza he goes
   inside to turn in his paperwork.

A brief mention of hazardous materials and the
   paperwork is signed correctly.
He's through; nothing to do but wait. He is lonely again.

In the mad dash of forklifts running east and west
The air thick with diesel smell, each worker is in their
   world, looking out
Through the grid of a cage and the blinding headlights
They think of home and the wife that sleeps alone in the
   bed that a truck brought.

TRANSIENT HOTEL SKY
AT THE HOUR OF SLEEP

Martín Espada

On the late shift, front desk,
midnight to eight AM,
we watched the sky through crusted windows,
till the clouds swirled away
like water in the drain
of a steel sink.

In the clouded liquid light
human shapes would harden,
an Army jacket staggering
against the bannister at bartime,
coalskinned man
drifting through the lobby
moaning to himself
about Mississippi,
a known arsonist
squeezing his head
in the microwave oven
with a giggle.

As we studied the white face
of the clock above the desk,
fluorescent hum of 4 AM,
a cowboy bragged
about buying good boots
for 19 cents from a retarded man,
then swaggered out the door
with a pickaxe
and a treasure map.
The janitor mopped the floor
nostalgic for Vietnam snapshots

confiscated at the airport,
peasant corpses with jaws
lopsided in a song of missing teeth.

Slowly the sky was a comfort,
like the pillow of a patient
sick for decades
and sleeping at last.
At the hour of sleep
a man called Johnson
trotted down the hallway
and leaned out the window,
then again, haunting
the fifth floor
in a staring litany
of gestures, so even
the security guard on rounds
wrote in the logbook for social workers
who never kept a schedule at night.
Johnson leaped
through the greasy pane of sky
at 5 AM,
refused suicide in flight,
and kicking struggled to stand in the air,
but snapped his ankles on the sidewalk
and burst his head on the curb,
scalp flapped open like the lid
on a bucket of red paint.

The newspaper shocked mouths
that day, but the transient hotel sky
drained pale as usual,
and someone pissed in the ashtray
by the desk, then leered
at the jabbering smokers.

THE BOUNCER'S CONFESSION

Martín Espada

I know about the Westerns
where stunt doubles bellyflop
through bannisters rigged to collapse
or crash through chairs designed to splinter.
A few times the job was like that.
A bone fragment still floats
in my right ring finger
because the human skull
is harder than any fist.

Mostly, I stood watch at the door
and imagined their skulls
brimming with alcohol
like divers drowning in their own helmets.
Their heads would sag, shaking
to stay awake, elbows sliding out
across the bar.
I gathered their coats. I found their hats.
I rolled up their paper bags
full of sacred objects only I could see.
I interrogated them for an address,
a hometown. I called the cab,
I slung an arm across my shoulders
to walk them down the stairs.

One face still wakes me some mornings.
I remember black-frame eyeglasses
off-balance, his unwashed hair.
I remember the palsy that made claws
of his hands, that twisted his mouth
in the trembling parody of a kiss.

I remember the stack of books he read
beside the beer he would not stop drinking.
I remember his fainted face
pressed against the bar.
This time, I dragged a corkscrewed body
slowly down the stairs, hugged to my ribs,
his books in my other hand,
only to see the impatient taxi
pulling away. I yelled at acceleration smoke,
then fumbled the body with the books
back up the stairs, and called the cab again.

No movie barrooms. No tall stranger
shot the body spread-eagled across the broken table.
No hero, with a hero's uppercut, knocked them out,
not even me. I carried them out.

ACCOUNTING

Linda France

If she traded in their hard currency,
she'd say sex is closer to death
than she'll ever let the johns get.
Though she'll do it without a second skin.
If they pay enough. If she's high enough.
A girl's got to keep herself. And love
doesn't come into it. She'll name her price,
see the colour of their money, make
a small killing she'll spend on crack.
And aren't the streets paved with it?

Just how old will she never own up to
when the man next door said to call
him *Uncle,* keep *their little secret?*
Behind the crack, a seven year old kid
shuts her eyes as the punter slams it in.
And her feet ache like fuck. On a good night,
a handful of blow-jobs in the back
of Japanese cars that make the sore
places at the sides of her mouth weep,
make her want to bite. But the crack
keeps her smiling. Who cares about dying?
She can't add up her life to much.

She drinks a lot of coffee. Four sugars.
On the streets at the end of a shift, thin,
hungover, she'll reckon she's a lucky tart,
with the luxury of a bed to fall into
and dream about her mother,
the colour of her eyes: moving pictures,
the words censored she can't afford.
One night will blur into another,
a few hours of daylight, the crack
between, the one thing that keeps her going.

FIRE

Wilfred Gibson

Across the Cleveland countryside the train
Panted and jolted through the lurid night
Of monstrous slag-heaps in the leaping light
Of belching furnaces: the driving rain
Lacing the glass with gold in that red glare
That momentarily revealed the cinderous land,
Of blasted fields, that stretched on either hand,
With livid waters gleaming here and there.

By hovels of men who labour till they die
With iron and the fire that never sleeps,
We plunged in pitchy night among huge heaps –
Then once again that red glare lit the sky
And high above the highest hill of slag
I saw Prometheus hanging from his crag.

NIGHT SHIFT

Karen Jane Glenn

Let us now praise the night shift –
those on the 8 to 4, the 10 to 6,
the 10-hour or 12-hour shift,
the bread bakers pounding and leavening,
the pastry cooks rolling and filling,
the sleep-deprived, the heavy-eyed,
the pale and dark ones sleeping
through their days, ambulance drivers
with their bright sirens, pilots
whose planes move like wandering stars,
the dawn-obsessed, the checkers of watches,
nurses slipping into unlit rooms,
the uniformed, the dressed-down, the truckers
with their high beams on, the wired,
the goosed up, the dragged down,
the lost and lonely selling tickets at dim windows,
girls who kick their shoes off, the ones
who walk the aisles, security staff, night watchmen,
all those who guard our nights,
unsmiling collectors of tolls, bouncers
at the after-hours bars, strummers
of guitars, ticklers of drums, working
in the shadow world where fluorescent lights
stand in for sun and flashes of neon
pass for stars. Let us praise the yawners
and those who stretch to stay awake,
coffee hounds, speed freaks, Coke drinkers,
women splashing water on their faces.
Remember the blackjack dealers with their gleaming cards,
waitresses sleepwalking from table to table,
taxi drivers with a gun in the glove,
all the weary, the fearful, the men

who never see their wives, the nervous babysitters,
those dancing to strange music, the clank
and drone of the factory machines,
printers rolling out the news,
all those dreaming of dawn and sleep
until, at last, in the first hint of light, the clerk
alone in the 7-11 counts the change in the cash drawer
and closes out the night.

NIGHTS AT THE MINE—
I'M ON SECURITY

John Harrison

It keeps changing
To something different,
Red sun, pink sea, the squeal of herring gulls.

Then mist makes the hill
Insubstantial, shifting. Sheep, you see them...
Then you don't.

The owner flew in, then taxi from Teesside,
Top bloke – from Israel,
Smiles for everyone.

One day he'll put this place back as it was,
Bulldoze the sheds,
Shot it all down the pit.

It turns out, life *is* cheery.
I was wrong.
Like t'owd gatehouse tom, I'm off on my rounds.

THE NIGHTWORKERS

Tobias Hill

Long after midnight
the railwaymen
work in pairs along the line
surreptitiously, at first,

the track stones
under their boots
trod like ice
into ruts.

The clocks stop for them.
Nothing comes
while they mend their ways.
Nothing goes. The night trains

rest in their stables.
The mainline lies
bright as cobweb

and the voice of the first man to speak
becomes a grand thing in the darkness
and the workers who follow
lope like so many bogeymen
through the lights of the gantry towers.

We lie awake for hours.
We rise like sleepers
hauled from beds of stone.
We cannot close our ears to the North
the railwaymen bring in their laughter.

Only towards morning will a word
turn them, one by one
homewards, calling names
and names and goodbyes as they go,

and though we'll be released to sleep
we'll lie awake in those small hours
until we're sure we've heard the last
there is to hear. We'll hang on their words,

listening for the lightness in them,
the lift in their voices at first light,
the eagerness they have in going home,
and even for the way they seem
to wake from sleep or dreams themselves,

as if they've slept their lives away, and now
find themselves boys again, waking in winter
to yell their names clear across miles of snow.

NIGHT WAITRESS

Lynda Hull

Reflected in the plate glass, the pies
look like clouds drifting off my shoulder.
I'm telling myself my face has character,
not beauty. It's my mother's Slavic face.
She washed the floor on hands and knees
below the Black Madonna, praying
to her god of sorrows and visions
who's not here tonight when I lay out the plates,
small planets, the cups and moons of saucers.
At this hour the men all look
as if they'd never had mothers.
They do not see me. I bring the cups.
I bring the silver. There's the man
who leans over the jukebox nightly
pressing the combinations
of numbers. I would not stop him
if he touched me, but it's only songs
of risky love he leans into. The cook sings
with the jukebox, a moan and sizzle
into the grill. On his forehead
a tattoed cross furrows,
diminished when he frowns. He sings words
dragged up from the bottom of his lungs.
I want a song that rolls
through the night like a big Cadillac
past factories to the refineries
squatting on the bay, round and shiny
as the coffee urn warming my palm.
Sometimes when coffee cruises my mind
visiting the most remote way stations,
I think of my room as a calm arrival
each book and lamp in its place. The calendar

on my wall predicts no disaster
only another white square waiting
to be filled like the desire that fills
jail cells, the cold arrest
that makes me stare out the window or want
to try every bar down the street.
When I walk out of here in the morning
my mouth is bitter with sleeplessness.
Men surge to the factories and I'm too tired
to look. Fingers grip lunch box handles,
belt buckles gleam, wind riffles my uniform
and it's not romantic when the sun unlids
the end of the avenue. I'm fading
in the morning's insinuations
collecting in the crevices of the building,
in wrinkles, in every fault
of this frail machinery.

NIGHT SHIFT IN THE RAIN

Tom Kelly

Car park's dead, bottle banks castle corners,
rain shuffles across empty spaces.

Shopping trolleys block Safeway's exit,
mongrels sniff for action,
high tail it behind the Co-op.

The security man adores TV,
knowing the hours he'll not live.

Then they arrive! Wearing rainbows
accuse grey,
from a world where melancholia is banned,
minor keys forcibly discouraged,
laughter, optimism obligatory.

Dog can't believe its luck-
reversed and made a God!

They begin to dance, bang drums,
outrageous coloured costumes,
flattering air,
play violins, guitars, such joyful music-
shopping trolleys clapping
a synchronised beat.

This transcendental moment evaporates,
the dog witnessed events,
his tail's unreliable.

The security man lost in a DVD,
the rest, us, too busy
watching rain attacking empty spaces.

PUB-BOOMING

Marilyn Longstaff

The rain that has been lashing down all day
has stopped, leaving the terraced streets glistening,
cobbles and slates like polished haematite

It's dark.
Intermittent street lamps spot our way.
Collecting tins over one arm,
bundle of 'War Cry' and 'Young Soldier' tucked under
   the other,
my little father and I push through the dark
to bring light to the drunken masses.

Uniformed, we walk to the bus stop,
catch the double decker to Stalybridge.
"We'll start in the Irish Club,
move on to the Working Men's Club",
rushing to sell our papers between the Bingo
and the 'turn'.

Down to the Travellers' Rest.
Dad sends me into the Saloon Bar alone,
"Hello love – you're a bit of alright."
"Come and sit on my knee."
"Better than the little wizened old bloke we usually get."
"My Dad," I say.

Back to Ashton to do Yates' Wine Lodge
before 11pm, and closing time.
The cockle man's not in tonight
so no precious packet of sea food for the Brigadier.
Our work over,
we join the fish shop queue, one on every corner here.

Clutching our news-wrapped parcels,
vinegar and chip fat seeping onto our fingers,
we make our way home, weary with heavy tins,
stinking of cigarette smoke, stale beer,
copper coins and vinegar.
I can smell it now.

THE FOUNDRY BOY

James Macfarlan

Mighty furnaces are flaring like a demon's breath of fire,
Forges like great burning cities break in many a crimson
                                                        spire;
Tongues of eager flame are lapping all the glory of the
                                                    heaven,
While a blush of burning hectic o'er the midnight's face
                                                    is driven.
Peals the thunder throat of Labour, hark! the deaf'ning
                                                anvils clash,
Like a thousand angry sabres in the battle's headlong
                                                        dash.
Hear the thoroughfares of tumult like the midnight
                                                Ocean's roar
As in agony he clutches at the black heart of the shore;
Toiling there the poor Boy-Poet grimes within a dismal
                                                        den,
Piles the fire and wields the hammer, jostled on by savage
                                                        men.
Burns his life to mournful ashes, on a thankless hearth of
                                                    gloom,
For a paltry pittance digging life from out an early tomb:
And the soul is dwarfed within him that was cast in Titan
                                                    mould,
And the wealth of Heaven he loses for the lack of human
                                                    gold,
And he cannot see the stars arise in splendid sheen of
                                                    light –
Like angel watchfires gleaming in the cloudy cliffs of night!

WEDNESDAY'S CHILD

Gary Ming

Exposed to every
wind driven drop,
no one likes working
in the rain;
even her

master of
gesture without
motion.

Wet enough to feel
colour wash from her flesh,
feel constriction in the rack
of her ribs, bone corset
crushing the heart.

A window drones down,
Radio 2 offers a world
she doesn't know

how much?

The question tugs her spine
that little bit tighter,
everything
moves in
that little bit tighter
crushing her heart
that little bit tighter.

FIGHTING FOAM

Kenn Mitchell

12 hours on the night shift
& fog stutters from the dark river.
mixes with vented steam from the paper machine
until there is no vision,
only the guttural moan of machines
that have an existence to merely produce.

i stand in that mix of fog & steam,
hosing the chemical reaction of pulp fiber, potato starch
& kyme (an additive to make paper
water resistant) known as foam –
a benign bubbling that is hosed inefficiently
into the sewer ... the procedure known as
fighting foam in the vernacular.

i look up & there stands
Cesar Vallejo in his blue suit,
no safety glasses, no hard hat –
obviously not in compliance
with safety regulations. i attempt
to explain, but he points to the moon
between fog banks & says something
in Spanish, which i do not understand.

he then steps back into the fog.
i do not follow
as the sound of alarms tells me
my distractions has let
the foam short out the trim squirt motors
& the paper machine is down.

i mutter to Vallejo:

"how the hell does that make you feel?"
not certain anyone can feel anything
at 3 in the morning, knowing
a mountain of paper work awaits the arrival
of the mill wide coordinator, who i am certain
is not wearing a neatly pressed blue suit.

RELEASE

Alan Morrison

Six Hundred hours Amen,
   All men
are free to clock-out
snail back home
in muttering cars
down empty roads
to beds warmed by
impressions of wives –
time to sink
into pillows for six
hours, dream better
things than shifts
and punished lives...

THE FORE SHIFT

Matthew Tate

Oh, the fore shift dark and dreary,
Oh, this lonely two o'clock;
Limbs may ache, and hearts be weary,
Still there comes the caller's knock;
And each blow upon the panels
Bids us up and don our flannels,
By the light of lamp or can'les
Batter at the grimy rock.

Just to get a bare subsistence,
Little earned and nothing saved,
With the workhouse in the distance
After we for years have slaved.
Some look on with holy horror,
At each pitman's little error,
But 'twould much abate their terror
Could they see the dangers braved.

To the coal's grim face we travel,
And again our flannels doff;
Can they wonder if we cavil
At the ones much better off?
Like a snake our bodies coiling,
Weary hours of incessant toiling,
Through each pore the sweat comes boiling;
Think on this, ye ones that scoff!

Up while stars are dimly peeping
Through the midnight's sable gloom;
Up while pampered ones are sleeping
In their snug and cosy room.

Fore shift visions need not haunt them,
Nor the pit's grim danger daunt them;
Oh, 'twas kind of fate to plant them
Where they could so safely bloom!

IN THE FORESTS
OF THE NIGHT

MOON FOX

Peter Bennett

A fox jumps off the wall and stabs
through snow across the rabbit ground.

His going is a sudden itch,
a tickle of the bandaged face
of moorland gawping at the moon.

He is the moon's familiar,
his brush the sickle's opposite.

THE TIGER

William Blake

Tiger! Tiger! burning bright
In the forests of the night,
What immortal hand or eye
Could frame thy fearful symmetry?

In what distant deeps or skies
Burned the fire of thine eyes?
On what wings dare he aspire?
What the hand dare seize the fire?

And what shoulder, and what art,
Could twist the sinews of thy heart?
And when thy heart began to beat,
What dread hand? And what dread feet?

What the hammer? What the chain?
In what furnace was thy brain?
What the anvil? What dread grasp
Dare its deadly terrors clasp?

When the stars threw down their spears,
And watered heaven with their tears,
Did he smile his work to see?
Did he who made the Lamb make thee?

Tiger! Tiger! burning bright
In the forests of the night,
What immortal hand or eye
Dare frame thy fearful symmetry?

SILVER

Walter de la Mare

Slowly, silently, now the moon
Walks the night in her silver shoon;
This way, and that, she peers, and sees
Silver fruit upon silver trees;
One by one the casements catch
Her beams beneath the silvery thatch;
Couched in his kennel, like a log,
With paws of silver sleeps the dog;
From their shadowy cote the white breasts peep
Of doves in a silver-feathered sleep;
A harvest mouse goes scampering by,
With silver claws and a silver eye;
And moveless fish in the water gleam,
By silver reeds in a silver stream.

from BADGER

John Clare

When midnight comes a host of dogs and men
Go out and track the badger to his den,
And put a sack within the hole, and lie
Till the old grunting badger passes by.
He comes and hears – they let the strongest loose.
The old fox hears the noise and drops the goose.
The poacher shoots and hurries from the cry,
And the old hare: half wounded buzzes by.
They get a forked stick to bear him down
And clap the dogs and take him to the town,
And bait him all the day with many dogs,
And laugh and shout and fright the scampering hogs.
He runs along and bites at all he meets:
They shout and hollo down the noisy streets.

He turns about to face the loud uproar
And drives the rebels to their very door.
The frequent stone is hurled where'er they go;
When badgers fight, then every one's a foe.
The dogs are clapt and urged to join the fray;
The badger turns and drives them all away.
Though scarcely half as big, demure and small,
He fights with dogs for hours and beats them all.
The heavy mastiff, savage in the fray,
Lies down and licks his feet and turns away.
The bulldog knows his match and waxes cold,
The badger grins and never leaves his hold.
He drives the crowd and follows at their heels
And bites them through – the drunkard swears and reels.

The frighted women take the boys away,
The blackguard laughs and hurries on the fray.
He tries to reach the woods, an awkward race,
But sticks and cudgels quickly stop the chase.
He turns agen and drives the noisy crowd
And beats the many dogs in noises loud.
He drives away and beats them every one,
And then they loose them all and set them on.
He falls as dead and kicked by boys and men,
Then starts and grins and drives the crowd agen;
Till kicked and torn and beaten out he lies
And leaves his hold and cackles, groans, and dies.

HARES AT PLAY

John Clare

The birds are gone to bed the cows are still
And sheep lie panting on each old mole hill
And underneath the willows grey green bough
Like toil a resting – lies the fallow plough
The timid hares throw daylights fears away
On the lanes road to dust and dance and play
Then dabble in the grain by nought deterred
To lick the dewfall from the barleys beard
Then out they sturt again and round the hill
Like happy thoughts dance squat and loiter still
Till milking maidens in the early morn
Gingle their yokes and start them in the corn
Through well known beaten paths each nimbling hare
Sturts quick as fear – and seeks its hidden lair

HOW WE GOT HOME

Josephine Dickinson

It was March, so it must have been spring,
but cold and the river was high,
bubbling like wine,
which I saw with the eyes
of the one who was close to death at the time,
but persisted, and therefore
they persisted with me
in my studied, clumsy course
on what was, admittedly,
a narrow path.
No evidence was later found
of the spot, nearly four fifths round,
we were forced to turn back.
No mark, no stick. We must have reached
a wordless core, for we turned in unison –
no need for the question where are you?
even on such pocked and dark terrain
and for such a length of time, time
being our language, as if the bridge
crossing provided all the compass or clock
we lacked, its structure an entrance,
its purpose defined by our unity, we three,
our common music which we carried
everywhere and asked with to cross
the first bridge again to the bank
which overlooks the Tyne and the Black Burn,
to turn there one last time...
                    This was Jack's last walk.
On the night he died I walked there with Hawthorne

at dusk. At Martins' Dive a frantic tussling
took the weeds at the edge of the path. Was it perhaps
an injured rabbitling? No, this creature snapped
side to side and tunnelled the grass,
cleared the path and the mush, then plopped
in the water, breathed and began its seamless passing.

RAINY MIDNIGHT

Ivor Gurney

Long shines the line of wet lamps dark in gleaming,
The trees so still felt yet as strength not used,
February chills April, the cattle are housed,
And nights grief from the higher things comes
    streaming.

The traffic is all gone, the elver-fishers gone
To string their lights 'long Severn like a wet Fair.
If it were fine the elvers would swim clear,
Clothes sodden, the out-of-work stay on.

AN AUGUST MIDNIGHT

Thomas Hardy

A shaded lamp and a waving blind,
And the beat of a clock from a distant floor:
On this scene enter – winged, horned, and spined –
A longlegs, a moth, and a dumbledore;
While 'mid my page there idly stands
A sleepy fly, that rubs its hands...

Thus meet we five, in this still place,
At this point of time, at this point in space.
– My guests besmear my new-penned line,
Or bang at the lamp and fall supine.
'God's humblest, they!' I muse. Yet why?
They know earth-secrets that know not I.

THE DARKLING THRUSH

Thomas Hardy

I leant upon a coppice gate
   When Frost was spectre-gray,
And Winter's dregs made desolate
   The weakening eye of day.
The tangled bine-stems scored the sky
   Like strings of broken lyres,
And all mankind that haunted nigh
   Had sought their household fires.

The land's sharp features seemed to be
   The Century's corpse outleant,
His crypt the cloudy canopy,
   The wind his death-lament.
The ancient pulse of germ and birth
   Was shrunken hard and dry,
And every spirit upon earth
   Seemed fervourless as I.

At once a voice arose among
   The bleak twigs overhead
In a full-hearted evensong
   Of joy illimited;
An aged thrush, frail, gaunt, and small,
   In blast-beruffled plume,
Had chosen thus to fling his soul
   Upon the growing gloom.

So little cause for carolings
   Of such ecstatic sound
Was written on terrestrial things
   Afar or nigh around,

That I could think there trembled through
   His happy good-night air
Some blessed Hope, whereof he knew
   And I was unaware.

THE NIGHT-PIECE TO JULIA

Robert Herrick

Her Eyes the Glow-worme lend thee,
  The Shooting Starres attend thee;
    And the Elves also,
    Whose little eyes glow,
Like the sparks of fire, befriend thee.

No *Will-o'th'-Wispe* mis-light thee;
  Nor Snake, or Slow-worme bite thee:
    Bat on, on thy way
    Not making a stay,
Since Ghost there's none to affright thee.

Let not the darke thee cumber;
  What though the Moon does slumber?
    The Starres of the night
    Will lend thee their light,
Like Tapers cleare without number.

Then *Julia* let me wooe thee,
  Thus, thus to come unto me:
    And when I shall meet
    Thy silv'ry feet,
My soule I'll poure into thee.

Hesperides, 1648

ODE TO A NIGHTINGALE

John Keats

My heart aches, and a drowsy numbness pains
  My sense, as though of hemlock I had drunk,
Or emptied some dull opiate to the drains
  One minute past, and Lethe-wards had sunk:
  'Tis not through envy of thy happy lot,
But being too happy in thy happiness,
    That thou, light-wingèd Dryad of the trees,
      In some melodious plot
  Of beechen green, and shadows numberless,
  Singest of summer in full-throated ease.

O for a draught of vintage! that hath been
  Cooled a long age in the deep-delved earth,
Tasting of Flora and the country-green,
  Dance, and Provençal song, and sunburnt mirth!
O for a beaker full of the warm South!
  Full of the true, the blushful Hippocrene,
    With beaded bubbles winking at the brim,
      And purple-stainèd mouth;
  That I might drink, and leave the world unseen,
  And with thee fade away into the forest dim:

Fade far away, dissolve, and quite forget
  What thou among the leaves hast never known,
The weariness, the fever, and the fret
  Here, where men sit and hear each other groan;
Where palsy shakes a few, sad, last grey hairs,
  Where youth grows pale, and spectre-thin, and dies;
    Where but to think is to be full of sorrow
      And leaden-eyed despairs;
  Where Beauty cannot keep her lustrous eyes,
  Or new Love pine at them beyond to-morrow.

Away! away! for I will fly to thee,
  Not charioted by Bacchus and his pards,
But on the viewless wings of Poesy,
  Though the dull brain perplexes and retards:
Already with thee! tender is the night,
  And haply the Queen-Moon is on her throne,
    Clustered around by all her starry Fays;
        But here there is no light,
  Save what from heaven is with the breezes blown
    Through verdurous glooms and winding mossy ways

I cannot see what flowers are at my feet,
  Nor what soft incense hangs upon the boughs,
But, in embalmed darkness, guess each sweet
  Wherewith the seasonable month endows
The grass, the thicket, and the fruit-tree wild;
  White hawthorn, and the pastoral eglantine;
    Fast fading violets covered up in leaves;
        And mid-May's eldest child,
  The coming musk-rose, full of dewy wine,
    The murmurous haunt of flies on summer eves.

Darkling I listen; and for many a time
  I have been half in love with easeful Death,
Called him soft names in many a musèd rhyme,
  To take into the air my quiet breath;
Now more than ever seems it rich to die,
  To cease upon the midnight with no pain,
While thou art pouring forth thy soul abroad
        In such an ecstasy!
  Still wouldst thou sing, and I have ears in vain –
To thy high requiem become a sod.

Thou wast not born for death, immortal Bird!
　No hungry generations tread thee down;
The voice I hear this passing night was heard
　In ancient days by emperor and clown:
Perhaps the self-same song that found a path
　Through the sad heart of Ruth, when, sick for home,
　　She stood in tears amid the alien corn;
　　　　　The same that oft times hath
　Charmed magic casements, opening on the foam
　Of perilous seas, in faery lands forlorn.

Forlorn! the very word is like a bell
　To toll me back from thee to my sole self!
Adieu! the fancy cannot cheat so well
　As she is famed to do, deceiving elf.
Adieu! adieu! thy plaintive anthem fades
　Past the near meadows, over the still stream,
　　Up the hill-side; and now 'tis buried deep
　　　　　In the next valley-glades:
　Was it a vision, or a waking dream?
　Fled is that music: – do I wake or sleep?

THE EEL-TRAP

Michael Longley

I lie awake and my mind goes out to the otter
That might be drowning in the eel-trap:
$\qquad\qquad\qquad\qquad\qquad$ your breathing
Falters as I follow you to the other lake
Below sleep, the brown trout sipping at the stars.

THE MOWER
TO THE GLOW-WORMS

Andrew Marvell

Ye living lamps, by whose dear light
The nightingale does sit so late,
And studying all the summer night,
Her matchless songs does meditate;

Ye country comets, that portend
No war, nor prince's funeral,
Shining unto no higher end
Than to presage the grass's fall;

Ye glow-worms, whose officious flame
To wandering mowers shows the way,
That in the night have lost their aim,
And after foolish fires do stray;

Your courteous lights in vain you waste,
Since *Juliana* here is come,
For she my mind hath so displaced
That I shall never find my home.

BAT VALLEY, KAMPALA

Graham Mort

You'll hear grasshoppers kindle their song, scratching
under palms beyond the mosque's gilt minaret where
slippers line up pale as lilies closing at the dusk.

Let's say a storm still billows at the western hills; there'll
be clouds of saffron bile, the sky fused-out, short-
circuiting in flickering blue effulgent sparks.

Roosting fruit bats flit from trees, loot last light, fly
from thunder's heat-charged columns to the sun-
spilled crimson of the lake's sheen.

The sky stammers bats: a host of sable tents,
torrent of invert light; their flux of dark spews
shadow on a dimming township's red dirt roads.

Sky sputters. The market breathes its scent of burnt
earth, plantain rot and diesel smoke, the cheeks of
maize-cob vendors etched by candles where you walk.

You watch those boys fade from the tennis court,
    returning
their lost ball when only bats should sense it scuffing
home from scooped half-volleys in the dusk.

They shake hands, slam their iron cage: *Go well.* The sky's
still flocculent with wings, the night a broth of dog howls,
storm-heat, sweat and insect-crackling grass.

Mosquitos blacken window mesh; moths' giant shadows
beat the lawn. Another drink: the glass cold, beer sharp
as constellations drawing current from the dark.

THE COYOTE

Paul Muldoon

Veering down the track like a girl veering down a
                                        cobbled street
in the meatpacking district,
high heels from the night before, black shawl of
                                        black-tipped hairs,

steering clear of that fluorescent ring
spray-painted on an even stretch of blacktop
like a ring in which we might once have played keepsies,

veering down the track without the slightest
                                acknowledgement from Angus,
the dog lying in a heap on our porch
like a heap of clothes lying beside a bed,

Angus who had himself been found wandering by the
                                        highway
somewhere on the far side of Lake Champlain,
slubber-furred, slammerkin, backbone showing through,

and, though we didn't know it when we brought him home,
blind in one eye, the right one,
the one between him and the coyote,

the cloudy, flaw-fleckered marble of that eye
now turning on you and me,
taking in the spray-painted ring where you and I
                                        knuckle down.

ATLAS MOTH

Pascale Petit

This giant atlas moth's broad wings
could be the map of China.

Here are two Great Walls. And there
on the Manchurian tip of each forewing

are dragon heads to scare off predators.
But what are those windows in the map,

where crystal scales let in the light?
As if earth's skin has windows

and at certain times of the evening
they open. The newly emerged atlas

perches on my hand, and it trembles –
like a new world, warming up for its first flight.

NIGHT

Miklós Radnóti

The heart is asleep and, in the heart, anxiety.
The fly is asleep near the cobweb on the wall.
The house is quiet: not a scratch from a wakeful mouse.
The garden sleeps, the branch, the woodpecker in the trunk,
The beetle sleeps in the rose, the bee in the hive
And summer in the wheat-grains that are scattering.
Flame sleeps in the moon too, cold medal on the sky.
Autumn is up and, to steal, goes stealthily by.

MOONRISE

Tom Rawling

Through darkness thicker than shadows,
the land lulled for predators,
my feet nudge the path to the pool.
I hear the splash of big fish
know they will come to my lure,
and for half an hour they do.
Then there is silent suspicion,
the nape of my neck prickles.

I turn to bushes just outlined,
a brightening sky, clouds breaking apart,
fingernail crescent coming clear
of the fells, lifting to spotlight
the stream. The land lies bleached,
pebbles pimple the shore, the water mirror
flashes my flailing arm, casting
alarm across the pool.

CONSTELLATIONS

Neil Rollinson

Beyond the house, where the woods
dwindle to a few stray trees, my father
Walks on the lake with a hammer.

He's never seen so many stars,
and wonders why
with all that light in the sky

it doesn't cast a single shadow.
He takes a few blows at the ice, and drops
a sackful of bricks

and kittens into the hole, listens
a moment to the stillness of deep winter,
the hugeness of sky, the bubbles of warm

oxygen breaking under his feet
like the fizz in a lemonade; the creaking
of ice as it settles itself.

His father's at home, coaxing voices
out of a crystal set, a concert from London.
Ghosts in a stone.

My father doesn't like that, he prefers
the magic of landscapes, of icicles
growing like fangs from the gutters of houses,

the map of the constellations. He turns on the bank
and looks at the sky, Orion rising over Bradford,
Cassiopeia's bold W, asking Who, What, When

and Why? And down in the lake, the sudden
star-burst of four kittens under a lid of ice,
heading to the four corners of nowhere.

70

NIGHT SNOW

Jane Routh

A light snow and it's explicit,
the history of the night.
Deer have betrayed their galleries and racks,
and crowded round high gates:
their slots depart, return, depart,
case the garden fence along the track.
The Y-pattern prints of a hare at speed
lengthen below a run through the hedge.
Four-toed runes of a heron's slow walk
track the heavy footed explorations of the geese.
Unreadable scuffs beneath the oak
and everything coming and going
along the path in Great Robin's Close,
grass showing through, and small things
going off-piste, familiar waymarks whited out.
Home, you used to say, but you
were always too hasty for any of this.

CALMING THE CAT AT MIDNIGHT
AFTER FIREWORKS

Derek Sellers

Tramping in pyjamas up and down the road,
I find and enfold him, after the terror hours.
Lamp-eyed, bristle-backed, he spent them
in the root-cage of a bush, in existential fear.
Now he emerges, aching from confinement,
but does not trust the quiet truce of midnight yet.

To ears attuned to the smallest sound – bird-
rustle, the scamper-pause-scamper of a mouse –
tonight's noises from the sky must have seemed
the anger of the gods. Even in my arms he quakes,
like a child-refugee from a war-zone, whose bones
shake with the aftershocks of guns and bombings.

This poem might have ended with a grander line –
'the thunderbolts of fate that make us cower....'
But rather not. Inappropriate to finish with a bang.
Instead, I offer this:
a man and a cat in moonlight on a roadway,
their shadows magnified, a leaf falling into the silence,
and, barely audible, the first tremblings of a purr.

THE BIRKDALE NIGHTINGALE
(*Bufo calamito* – the Natterjack toad)

Jean Sprackland

On Spring nights you can hear them
two miles away, calling their mates
to the breeding place, a wet slack in the dunes.
Lovers hiding nearby are surprised
by desperate music. One man searched all night
for a crashed spaceship.

For amphibians, they are terrible swimmers:
where it's tricky to get ashore, they drown.
By day they sleep in crevices under the boardwalk,
run like lizards from cover to cover
without the sense to leap when a gull snaps.
Yes, he can make himself fearsome,
inflating his lungs to double his size.
But cars on the coast road are not deterred.

She will lay a necklace of pearls in the reeds.
Next morning, a dog will run into the water and scatter
    them.
Or she'll spawn in a footprint filled with salt rain
that will dry to a crust in two days.

Still, when he calls her and climbs her
they are well designed. The nuptial pads on his thighs
velcro him to her back. She steadies beneath him.

The puddle brims with moonlight.
Everything leads to this.

NIGHT WALKING WITH SHADOWS

Anne Stevenson

Night walking the dog through the hollow village,
I am followed and preceded by three of me.

The streetlights distribute me between three shamans.
Their huge imaginations hand me, like a trophy,
from the shadow behind me to the shadow before me.

While the full moon gives me a dense
practical shadow, smaller than myself.

I walk, for the dog's sake, out of the lights
up the track by the sportsground, the shacky allotments.

How this white fall of moonlight simplifies the story.
Dog and shadow. Woman and shadow.

Up the V of the valley, a string of brilliants.
In every window, labouring magi.

The chimney pots steam like alembics,
but for every white chain of amazing smoke,
the moon cuts a dead black track.

THE BAT

Matthew Sweeney

In through the open French window
Flew the bat, past my head
As I stood peeing into the river
That flowed beneath the house
Which the bat quickly explored, round
The barn-sized living-room,
Up the cracked stairs, two flights
To the attic where the kids slept
But they wouldn't tonight, not while
The bat stayed. So we opened
The skylight, despite the wasp's nests
On the drainpipe, and I stood
With a glass of the local red wine,
Calling to the bat, like Dracula,
Lovely creature of the night,
Come to me, I am your friend,
While it looped the length of the room,
With the kids on the stairs, laughing,
But not coming in. And it stayed
Past midnight, till Joan
Cupped it in her hands
And carried it downstairs
To the same French window,
Where I stood, calling after it,
Lovely creature of the night,
Come back, I miss you,
Come to me, I am your friend.

OUT IN THE DARK

Edward Thomas

Out in the dark over the snow
The fallow fawns invisible go
With the fallow doe;
And the winds blow
Fast as the stars are slow.

Stealthily the dark haunts round
And, when the lamp goes, without sound
At a swifter bound
Than the swiftest hound,
Arrives, and all else is drowned;

And I and star and wind and deer,
Are in the dark together, – near,
Yet far, – and fear
Drums on my ear
In that sage company drear.

How weak and little is the light,
All the universe of sight,
Love and delight,
Before the might,
If you love it not, of night.

THE OWL

Edward Thomas

Downhill I came, hungry, and yet not starved;
Cold, yet had heat within me that was proof
Against the North wind; tired, yet so that rest
Had seemed the sweetest thing under a roof.

Then at the inn I had food, fire, and rest,
Knowing how hungry, cold, and tired was I.
All of the night was quite barred out except
An owl's cry, a most melancholy cry

Shaken out long and clear upon the hill,
No merry note, nor cause of merriment,
But one telling me plain what I escaped
And others could not, that night, as in I went.

And salted was my food, and my repose,
Salted and sobered, too, by the bird's voice
Speaking for all who lay under the stars,
Soldiers and poor, unable to rejoice.

THE NATURALIST'S
SUMMER EVENING WALK

...equidem credo, quia sit divinitus illis ingenium.
(Virgil)

Gilbert White

When day declining sheds a milder gleam,
What time the may-fly haunts the pool or stream;
When the still owl skims round the grassy mead,
What time the timorous hare limps forth to feed;
Then be the time to steal adown the vale,
And listen to the vagrant cuckoo's tale;
To hear the clamorous curlew call his mate,
Or the soft quail his tender pain relate;
To see the swallow sweep the dark'ning plain
Belated, to support her infant train;
To mark the swift in rapid giddy ring
Dash round the steeple, unsubdu'd of wing:
Amusive birds! – say where your hid retreat
When the frost rages and the tempests beat;
Whence your return, by such nice instinct led
When spring, soft season, lifts her bloomy head?
Such baffled searches mock man's prying pride,
The God of Nature is your secret guide!

While deep'ning shades obscure the face of day,

To yonder bench leaf-shelter'd let us stray,
Till blended objects fail the swimming sight,
And all the facing landscape sinks in night;

To hear the drowsy dor* come brushing by
With buzzing wing, or the shrill cricket cry;
To see the feeding bat glance through the wood;
To catch the distant falling of the flood;
While o'er the cliff th'awaken'd churn-owl hung
Through the still gloom protracts his chattering song;
While high in air, and pois'd upon his wings,
Unseen, the soft enamour'd woodlark stags:
These, Nature's works, the curious mind employ,
Inspire a soothing melancholy joy:
As fancy warms a pleasing kind of pain
Steals o'er the cheek, and thrills the creeping vein!

Each rural sight, each sound, each smell combine;

The tinkling sheep-bell, or the breath of kine;
The new-mown hay that scents the swelling breeze,
Or cottage-chimney smoking through the trees.

The chilling night-dews fall: – away, retire;

For see, the glow-worm lights her amorous fire!
Thus, e'er night's veil had half obscur'd the sky,
Th'impatient damsel hung her lamp on high:
True to the signal, by love's meteor led,
Leander hastened to his Hero's bed.

* *beetle*

BEWICK SWANS ARRIVE AT OUSE WASHES

Lynne Wycherley

Just when I think the winter has won,
a black book closing

on pages of light,
and the darkness sways on its haunches

like an impatient bear
scooping up silver minnows,

I sense an agitation in the sky,
long Vs trailing like pennons,

Altocirrus, swans white
as the tundra they come from.

Their cries multiply. Their bodies
crash-land on the water

star after star after star.

THE WILD SWANS AT COOLE
(Coole Park, Galway)

W.B. Yeats

The trees are in their autumn beauty,
The woodland paths are dry,
Under the October twilight the water
Mirrors a still sky,
Upon the brimming water among the stones
Are nine-and-fifty swans.

The nineteenth autumn has come upon me
Since I first made my count;
I saw, before I had well finished,
All suddenly mount
And scatter wheeling in great broken rings
Upon their clamorous wings.

I have looked upon those brilliant creatures,
And now my heart is sore.
All's changed since I, hearing at twilight,
The first time on this shore,
The bell-beat of their wings above my head,
Trod with a lighter tread.

Unwearied still, lover by lover,
They paddle in the cold
Companionable streams or climb the air;
Their hearts have not grown old;
Passion or conquest, wander where they will,
Attend upon them still.

But now they drift on the still water,
Mysterious, beautiful;
Among what rushes will they build,
By what lake's edge or pool
Delight men's eyes when I awake some day
To find they have flown away?

THE CRUMPLED DUVET

THINGS

Fleur Adcock

There are worse things than having behaved foolishly in
    public.
There are worse things than these miniature betrayals,
committed or endured or suspected; there are worse
    things
than not being able to sleep for thinking about them.
It is 5am. All the worse things come stalking in
and stand icily about the bed looking worse and worse
    and worse.

NIGHT SHIFT

Simon Armitage

Once again I have missed you by moments;
steam hugs the rim of the just-boiled kettle,

water in the pipes finds its own level.
In another room there are other signs

of someone having left: dust, unsettled
by the sweep of the curtains; the clockwork

contractions of the paraffin heater.
For weeks now we have come and gone, woken

in acres of empty bedding, written
lipstick love-notes on the bathroom mirror

and in this space we have worked and paid for
we have found ourselves, but lost each other.

Upstairs, at least, there is understanding
in things more telling than lipstick kisses:

the air, still hung with spores of your hairspray;
body-heat stowed in the crumpled duvet.

DOVER BEACH

Matthew Arnold

The sea is calm tonight.
The tide is full, the moon lies fair
Upon the straits; on the French coast the light
Gleams and is gone; the cliffs of England stand,
Glimmering and vast, out in the tranquil bay.
Come to the window, sweet is the night-air!
Only, from the long line of spray
Where the sea meets the moon-blanched land,
Listen! you hear the grating roar
Of pebbles which the waves draw back, and fling,
At their return, up the high strand,
Begin, and cease, and then again begin
With tremulous cadence slow, and bring
The eternal note of sadness in.

Sophocles long ago
Heard it on the Aegean, and it brought
Into his mind the turbid ebb and flow
Of human misery; we
Find also in the sound a thought,
Hearing it by this distant northern sea.

The Sea of Faith
Was once, too, at the full, and round earth's shore
Lay like the folds of a bright girdle furled.
But now I only hear
Its melancholy, long, withdrawing roar,
Retreating, to the breath
Of the night-wind, down the vast edges drear
And naked shingles of the world.

Ah, love, let us be true
To one another! for the world, which seems
To lie before us like a land of dreams,
So various, so beautiful, so new,
Hath really neither joy, nor love, nor light,
Nor certitude, nor peace, nor help for pain;
And we are here as on a darkling plain
Swept with confused alarms of struggle and flight,
Where ignorant armies clash by night.

HERE COMES NIGHT
after Baudelaire's "Le Crépuscule du Soir"

translated by John Lucas

Here comes night, good friend to the criminal,
a shadowy time when man turns frankly feral
as dark draws close like curtains round a bed
and light's shut out, the day's hours left for dead.

The evening can't come soon enough for all
whose aching limbs tell them that they're in thrall
to work's hard grip, must drudge to earn a crust
before they're freed into that sleep of the just
denied to grief-tossed sufferers, mute, tear-vexed,
or bug-eyed scholars labouring at a text.
Now black, lumpish demons take to the sky,
suited for business, thump against shutters, try
door-knobs, mutter down flues, make windows shake
in wind that trembles gas-jets as poor girls take
their first illuminated steps; now whores
swarm on the streets from out a thousand doors,
thronged myrmidons whose planned surprise attack
is like a secret army's, right on track
to steer a path through slime-streaked city ways
tainting all that it breathes on, touches, tastes.
From kitchens you can hear some tuneless whistle,
the theatre's hubbub, drum rolls, violins' snivel;
and then the pubs where board games guarantee
full tables for slick gamblers, on each knee
a fur-wrapped moll, while crooks and thieves look on,
about to try their night skills on the town,
merciless when they spring each safe to rifle
through drawers for gold and jewels, reserve a trifle
for Dawn or Char. (The girls must be kept sweet
some few days till they're sent back on the street.)

Faced with this turbid hour, turn inward, soul,
and stop your ears against its roar, the roil
of noise that's thickened by sick people's groans
as night seizes their throats and stills their moans.
Their last sighs fill the wards. Few from this group
of invalids will sip his hearth-side soup
ever again, such fragrant soup, and warm
as the loved one who filled and lit his home.

Though to be sure, most, going without a wife
or home's solace, are exiled from this life.

3AM FEED

Steven Blyth

Soon we abandoned our "turns". I volunteered
Finding that, alone, the world hushed, I could almost hear

It whispered – "This is your son."

In the crook of my arm, a perfect fit,
You were those words given weight.

Your fish mobiles made it seem we sat on the sea bed,

Your bottle a little oxygen tank,
Your gentle sucking like a tick, tick, tick

Timing how long before we had to go up,

Face currents that tugged us apart – the fuss
Of want-to-hold relatives and, worse, the office

That kept me from your first step, first clear word.

Those moments were in the presence of grandparents
    and mum,
Remembered in detail – *Ten past one,*

Blur on the radio; he went from the armchair

To the coffee table. Still, for me,
Those feeds have equal clarity,

Last week coming so strongly to mind –

Caught T-shirted in a summer storm,
My forearm felt drops as large and warm

As the one I'd splash there to test the temperature.

That white drop would sometimes dribble
Down to my palm – a pearl.

NIGHT FEED

Eavan Boland

This is dawn.
Believe me
This is your season, little daughter.
The moment daisies open,
The hour mercurial rainwater
Makes a mirror for sparrows.
It's time we drowned our sorrows.

I tiptoe in.
I lift you up
Wriggling
In your rosy, zipped sleeper.
Yes, this is the hour
For the early bird and me
When finder is keeper.

I crook the bottle.
How you suckle!
This is the best I can be,
Housewife
To this nursery
Where you hold on,
Dear Life.

A silt of milk.
The last suck.
And now your eyes are open,
Birth-coloured and offended.
Earth wakes.
You go back to sleep.
The feed is ended.

Worms turn.
Stars go in.
Even the moon is losing face
Poplars stilt for dawn
And we begin
The long fall from grace
I tuck you in.

from DON JUAN, Canto II

Lord Byron

They look upon each other and their eyes
Gleam in the moonlight; and her white arm clasps
Round Juan's head, and his around her lies
Half buried in the tresses which it grasps;
She sits upon his knee, and drinks his sighs,
He hers, until they end in broken gasps;
And thus they form a group that's quite antique,
Half naked, loving, natural, and Greek.

And when those deep and burning moments pass'd,
And Juan sunk to sleep within her arms,
She slept not, but all tenderly, though fast,
Sustain'd his head upon her bosom's charms;
And now and then her eye to heaven is cast,
And then on the pale cheek her breast now warms,
Pillow'd on her o'erflowing heart, which pants
With all it granted, and with all it grants.

...The lady watch'd her lover – and that hour
Of Love's, and Night's, and Ocean's solitude,
O'erflowed her soul with their united power;
Amidst the barren sand and rocks so rude
She and her wave-born love had made their bower,
Where nought upon their passion could intrude,
And all the stars that crowded the blue space
Saw nothing happier than her glowing face.

FROST AT MIDNIGHT

Samuel Taylor Coleridge

The Frost performs its secret ministry,
Unhelped by any wind. The owlet's cry
Came loud – and hark, again! loud as before.
The inmates of my cottage, all at rest,
Have left me to that solitude, which suits
Abstruser musings: save that at my side
My cradled infant slumbers peacefully.
'Tis calm indeed! so calm, that it disturbs
And vexes meditation with its strange
And extreme silentness. Sea, hill, and wood,
This populous village! Sea, and hill, and wood,
With all the numberless goings-on of life,
Inaudible as dreams! the thin blue flame
Lies on my low-burnt fire, and quivers not;
Only that film, which fluttered on the grate,
Still flutters there, the sole unquiet thing.
Methinks, its motion in this hush of nature
Gives it dim sympathies with me who live,
Making it a companionable form,
Whose puny flaps and freaks the idling Spirit

By its own moods interprets, every where
Echo or mirror seeking of itself,
And makes a toy of Thought.

　　　　　But O! how oft,
How oft, at school, with most believing mind,
Presageful, have I gazed upon the bars,
To watch that fluttering *stranger!* and as oft
With unclosed lids, already had I dreamt
Of my sweet birth-place, and the old church-tower,
Whose bells, the poor man's only music, rang
From morn to evening, all the hot Fair-day,
So sweetly, that they stirred and haunted me
With a wild pleasure, falling on mine ear
Most like articulate sounds of things to come!
So gazed I, till the soothing things, I dreamt,
Lulled me to sleep, and sleep prolonged my dreams!
And so I brooded all the following morn,
Awed by the stern preceptor's face, mine eye
Fixed with mock study on my swimming book:
Save if the door half opened, and I snatched
A hasty glance, and still my heart leaped up,
For still I hoped to see the *stranger's* face,
Townsman, or aunt, or sister more beloved,
My play-mate when we both were clothed alike!

Dear Babe, that sleepest cradled by my side,
Whose gentle breathings, heard in this deep calm,
Fill up the interspersèd vacancies
And momentary pauses of the thought!
My babe so beautiful! it thrills my heart
With tender gladness, thus to look at thee,
And think that thou shalt learn far other lore,
And in far other scenes! For I was reared
In the great city, pent 'mid cloisters dim,
And saw nought lovely but the sky and stars.

But *thou,* my babe! shalt wander like a breeze
By lakes and sandy shores, beneath the crags
Of ancient mountain, and beneath the clouds,
Which image in their bulk both lakes and shores
And mountain crags: so shalt thou see and hear
The lovely shapes and sounds intelligible
Of that eternal language, which thy God
Utters, who from eternity doth teach
Himself in all, and all things in himself.
Great universal Teacher! he shall mould
Thy spirit, and by giving make it ask.

Therefore all seasons shall be sweet to thee,
Whether the summer clothe the general earth
With greenness, or the redbreast sit and sing
Betwixt the tufts of snow on the bare branch
Of mossy apple-tree, while the nigh thatch
Smokes in the sun-thaw; whether the eave-drops fall
Heard only in the trances of the blast,
Or if the secret ministry of frost
Shall hang them up in silent icicles,
Quietly shining to the quiet Moon.

CITY EVENING

Frances Cornford

This is the hour when night says to the streets:
'I am coming'; and the light is so strange
The heart expects adventure in everything it meets;
Even the past to change.

THE LISTENERS

Walter de la Mare

"Is there anybody there?" said the Traveller,
    Knocking on the moonlit door;
And his horse in the silence champed the grasses
    Of the forest's ferny floor.
And a bird flew up out of the turret,
    Above the Traveller's head:
And he smote upon the door a second time;
    "Is there anybody there?" he said.
But no one descended to the Traveller;
    No head from the leaf-fringed sill
Leaned over and looked into his grey eyes,
    Where he stood perplexed and still.
But only a host of phantom listeners
    That dwelt in the lone house then
Stood listening in the quiet of the moonlight
    To that voice from the world of men:
Stood thronging the faint moonbeams on the dark stair
    That goes down to the empty hall,
Hearkening in an air stirred and shaken
    By the lonely Traveller's call.
And he felt in his heart their strangeness,
    Their stillness answering his cry,
While his horse moved, cropping the dark turf,
    'Neath the starred and leafy sky;
For he suddenly smote the door, even
    Louder, and lifted his head: –
"Tell them I came, and no one answered,
    That I kept my word," he said.
Never the least stir made the listeners,
    Though every word he spake
Fell echoing through the shadowiness of the still house
    From the one man left awake:

Ay, they heard his foot upon the stirrup,
  And the sound of iron on stone,
And how the silence surged softly backward,
  When the plunging hoofs were gone.

WILD NIGHTS

Emily Dickinson

Wild Nights – Wild Nights!
Were I with thee
Wild Nights should be
Our luxury!

Futile – the Winds –
To a Heart in port –
Done with the Compass –
Done with the Chart!

Rowing in Eden –
Ah, the Sea!
Might I but moor – Tonight –
In Thee!

NIGHT DRIVING

Maura Dooley

Across the Pennines maybe, at first frost,
when your headlamps make milky the way ahead,

or approaching Toronto at 4.00am
when stars lie scattered on the still lake,

driving fast, the windows pulled down,
to let the night winds steady your hands

you're tuned into strange stations
playing old hits you wish you didn't know.

Turning a dial fills the air with static:
oceans, the blueness of night

and you own the road, the country.
The radio speaks only to you.

A CHILD'S SLEEP

Carol Ann Duffy

I stood at the edge of my child's sleep
hearing her breathe;
although I could not enter there,
I could not leave.

Her sleep was a small wood,
perfumed with flowers;
dark, peaceful, sacred,
acred in hours.

And she was the spirit that lives
in the heart of such woods;
without time, without history,
wordlessly good.

I spoke her name, a pebble dropped
in the still night
and saw her stir, open both palms
cupping their soft light;

then went to the window. The greater dark
outside the room
gazed back, maternal, wise,
with its face of moon.

PRAYER

Elaine Feinstein

The windows are black tonight. The lamp
at my bedside peering with its yellow
40 watt light can hardly make out the chair.
Nothing is stranger than the habit of prayer.

The face of God as seen on this planet
is rarely gentle: the young gazelle is food
for the predator; filmy shapes
that need little more than carbon and water,

evolve like patterns on Dawkins'
computer; the intricate miracles
of eye and wing respond to the same
logic. I accept the evidence.

God is the wish to live. Everywhere,
as carnivores lick their young with
tenderness, in the human struggle
nothing is stranger than the habit of prayer.

THE NIGHT CITY

W.S. Graham

Unmet at Euston in a dream
Of London under Turner's steam
Misting the iron gantries, I
Found myself running away
From Scotland into the golden city.

I ran down Gray's Inn Road and ran
Till I was under a black bridge.
This was me at nineteen
Late at night arriving between
The buildings of the City of London.

And then I (O I have fallen down)
Fell in my dream beside the Bank
Of England's wall to bed, me
With my money belt of Northern ice.
I found Eliot and he said yes

And sprang into a Holmes cab.
Boswell passed me in the fog
Going to visit Whistler who
Was with John Donne who had just seen
Paul Potts shouting on Soho Green.

> Midnight. I hear the moon
> Light chiming on St Paul's.

> The City is empty. Night
> Watchmen are drinking their tea.

The Fire had burnt out.
The Plague's pits had closed
And gone into literature.

Between the big buildings
I sat like a flea crouched
In the stopped works of a watch.

SLEEPING BIN BAGS

Atar Hadari

Huddled but snug against the brick
these bin bags powdered by the snow
await the morning men with no regrets
as if asleep on some forgiving stone.

And every wind lifts them
slightly off of the street –
the wind rustles their wrinkled heads
the rubbish bags asleep like kids.

And every time some wind idles,
lifts their rustling fur
they settle again to their shared glints
they wrinkle without a groan

and every powdered snowflake
falling on them in the gleam
of sodium gold is like a claim
of some permanence in this half home.

The bin bags by the street
wait as if there is time
and whistling someone comes
to whisk them off – light as old love, yesterday's arms.

NIGHT

Mark Haworth-Booth

We lie in bed and try to place the voices,
remembering our early-marriage rows.

'I work', or something, he mumbles, drunk.
'But I work', his wife replies, 'I w-o-r-k',

her vowels long and clear and thrilling
under the plane tree and street lamp,

like a speech by Sonia in *Vanya*.
She taunts him as he kicks their door in.

'Oh ma-cho, ma-cho man.'
He bangs at something else as they go in,

almost like a gun.
No scream, nothing breaks.

We wait without a sound.
In the bedroom through the party wall

the woman starts to cry, to whimper.
It's like a perfect telephone connection,

the sound of someone hit,
sitting on a bed, head in her hands,

maybe trying to be sick.
The gasps, the moans and almost laugh,

like overhearing sex.
A volley from the door downstairs. The man

hammers at the hinges of his marriage
with all the passion that he can.

AUBADE

Philip Larkin

I work all day, and get half-drunk at night.
Waking at four to soundless dark, I stare.
In time the curtain-edges will grow light.
Till then I see what's really always there:
Unresting death, a whole day nearer now,
Making all thought impossible but how
And where and when I shall myself die.
Arid interrogation: yet the dread
Of dying, and being dead,
Flashes afresh to hold and horrify.

The mind blanks at the glare. Not in remorse
– The good not done, the love not given, time
Torn off unused – nor wretchedly because
An only life can take so long to climb
Clear of its wrong beginnings, and may never;
But at the total emptiness for ever,
The sure extinction that we travel to
And shall be lost in always. Not to be here,
Not to be anywhere,
And soon; nothing more terrible, nothing more true.

This is a special way of being afraid
No trick dispels. Religion used to try,
That vast moth-eaten musical brocade
Created to pretend we never die,
And specious stuff that says *No rational being
Can fear a thing it will not feel,* not seeing
That this is what we fear – no sight, no sound,
No touch or taste or smell, nothing to think with,
Nothing to love or link with,
The anaesthetic from which none come round.

And so it stays just on the edge of vision,
A small unfocused blur, a standing chill
That slows each impulse down to indecision.
Most things may never happen: this one will,
And realisation of it rages out
In furnace-fear when we are caught without
People or drink. Courage is no good:
It means not scaring others. Being brave
Lets no one off the grave.
Death is no different whined at than withstood.

Slowly light strengthens, and the room takes shape.
It stands plain as a wardrobe, what we know,
Have always known, know that we can't escape,
Yet can't accept. One side will have to go.
Meanwhile telephones crouch, getting ready to ring
In locked-up offices, and all the uncaring
Intricate rented world begins to rouse.
The sky is white as clay, with no sun.
Work has to be done.
Postmen like doctors go from house to house.

NIGHT-WATCH MAN & MUSE

Mark Murphy

I watch over the town like a lost angel
just beginning to grasp the significance of my task.
Where ever you are asleep, I hear the sounds
of sleep-walkers, sleep-talkers and sleep-junkies – too
    tired
to mutter more than the odd syllable about growing old,
reciting the names of ex-lovers and sweet-hearts
as though their litanies would bring back
the lost, the wounded, the deceased
for that one last conversation that would change
    everything.
They talk the honest talk of the subconscious mind
(allowing as we do for the affairs of translation)
and we must congratulate them on their night babble.
Never again will Jill tell Jack the truth – only in dreams.
And what of the truth, undependable as it is, changeable
as always by the way the light catches valleys and peaks.
My task is simply to watch and listen whilst
the last of the party goers take themselves home
and the very last stragglers, who have lost their sense
of what is right and wrong, think their way
into the bedrooms of the handsome and the beautiful.
I do not seek to order the night, I hear the lonely,
the sick, the maligned, the disparate voices
of a town groaning under the weight its own
    contradictions
and offer comfort in the long hours when no other voice
but the stranger's voice on the phone will do.

INSOMNIAC

Sylvia Plath

The night sky is only a sort of carbon paper,
Blueblack, with the much-poked periods of stars
Letting in the light, peephole after peephole –
A bonewhite light, like death, behind all things.
Under the eyes of the stars and the moon's rictus
He suffers his desert pillow, sleeplessness
Stretching its fine, irritating sand in all directions.

Over and over the old, granular movie
Exposes embarrassments – the mizzling days
Of childhood and adolescence, sticky with dreams,
Parental faces on tall stalks, alternately stern and tearful,
A garden of buggy roses that made him cry.
His forehead is bumpy as a sack of rocks.
Memories jostle each other for face-room like obsolete film
    stars.

He is immune to pills: red, purple, blue –
How they lit the tedium of the protracted evening!
Those sugary planets whose influence won for him
A life baptised in no-life for a while,
And the sweet, drugged waking of a forgetful baby.
Now the pills are worn-out and silly, like classical gods.
Their poppy-sleepy colours do him no good.

His head is a little interior of grey mirrors.
Each gesture flees immediately down an alley
Of diminishing perspectives, and its significance
Drains like water out the hole at the far end.
He lives without privacy in a lidless room,
The bald slots of his eyes stiffened wide-open
On the incessant heat-lightning flicker of situations.

Nightlong, in the granite yard, invisible cats
Have been howling like women, or damaged instruments.
Already he can feel daylight, his white disease,
Creeping up with her hatful of trivial repetitions.
The city is a map of cheerful twitters now,
And everywhere people, eyes mica-silver and blank,
Are riding to work in rows, as if recently brainwashed.

SHEFFIELD BY NIGHT

Peter Sansom

After the nightclubs have turned out and before
the cleaners have plugged in, the city is as still
as a snowglobe this last day of summer.
I sweat up Paradise St that was Workhouse Rd
and out under green-lit trees of the cathedral
like strolling through an artist's impression;
then over new tramtracks that dad would know
as far as the Cutler's Hall and HSBC.
A dog walking itself in the corner of my eye
past Pollards is gone before I see it's a fox.
Next, Boots the Chemists bright as a cruise ship
but the Marie Celeste; then over Fargate
and down Chapel Walk, the Link, the Samaritans,
and double-take at shoes a month's wages;
past the delivery-end of M&S now turn left
by the Crucible. I'm not mugged
in the subway or offered sex to feed a habit.
Ghost roadworks on the steep bit of Flat Street
and in the waking Interchange Paul Simon's
got that ticket still for his destination.
The Grade II listed eyesore on the skyline
is a memory of the Socialist Republic
and in its people-centred daring typical
of Sheaf Field, home of the cyclepath and bendi-
bus, the most wooded city in Europe if you
don't listen to Brum, and the most parks too,
that turned the steelworks into a shopping centre,
and the shopping centre into another world –
then suddenly here, at what I think of as Midland Station
to carry this lightheaded flu to Nottingham.

A NUMINOUS EVENT

Vernon Scannell

Only once in my life have I experienced
A numinous event. God spoke to me.
I do not mean this metaphorically
Or by dream or through Urim or a prophet
But that He spoke to me with a physical voice
Which issued from the mystery beyond
The dark sky and its white rash of stars
On a frosty night on Ealing Broadway.
I stood transfixed, amazed, my face raised
To feel a silvery beatitude descend.

I don't remember the exact words uttered
Nor could I honestly describe the voice
Except that I would swear that it was male.
But this I do recall with total certainty:
The tone was benevolent and reassuring.
Church bells began to roll and tremble in the skies
For it was Christmas Eve and all the pubs
Had extensions of their licenses.

I think God was forgiving me for my absence
From His mass. I know that He spoke to me,
Although the words themselves are lost
Or, if not lost, are hidden in the mist
Of almost half a century. And yes,
I must confess,
I might have been at least a little pissed.

from IN MEMORIAM

Alfred, Lord Tennyson

Dark house, by which once more I stand
  Here in the long unlovely street,
  Doors, where my heart was used to beat
So quickly, waiting for a hand,

A hand that can be clasp'd no more
  Behold me, for I cannot sleep,
  And like a guilty thing I creep
At earliest morning to the door.

He is not here; but far away
  The noise of life begins again,
  And ghastly thro' the drizzling rain
On the bald street breaks the blank day.

from UNDER MILK WOOD

Dylan Thomas

To begin at the beginning:
It is spring, moonless night in the small town, starless
and bible-black, the cobblestreets silent and the
hunched, courters'-and-rabbits' wood limping invisible
down to the sloeblack, slow, black, crowblack,
fishingboat-bobbing sea. The houses are blind as moles
(though moles see fine tonight in the snouting, velvet
dingles) or blind as Captain Cat there in the muffled
middle by the pump and the town clock, the shops in
mourning, the Welfare Hall in widows' weeds. And all
the people of the lulled and dumbfound town are
sleeping now.

Hush, the babies are sleeping, the farmers, the
fishers, the tradesmen and pensioners, cobbler,
schoolteacher, postman and publican, the undertaker
and the fancy woman, drunkard, dressmaker, preacher,
policeman, the webfoot cocklewomen and the tidy wives.
Young girls lie bedded soft or glide in their dreams, with
rings and trousseaux, bridesmaided by glow-worms
down the aisles of the organplaying wood. The boys are
dreaming wicked or of the bucking ranches of the night
and the jollyrodgered sea. And the anthracite statues of
the horses sleep in the fields, and the cows in the byres,
and the dogs in the wetnosed yards; and the cats nap in
the slant corners or lope sly, streaking and needling, on
the one cloud of the roofs.

You can hear the dew falling, and the hushed town
breathing. Only *your* eyes are unclosed, to see the black
and folded town fast, and slow, asleep. And you alone
can hear the invisible starfall, the darkest-before-dawn
minutely dewgrazed stir of the black, dab-filled sea
where the *Arethusa,* the *Curlew* and the *Skylark,*

Zanzibar, Rhiannon, the *Rover,* the *Cormorant,* and the
Star of Wales tilt and ride.

Listen. It is night moving in the streets, the
processional salt slow musical wind in Coronation Street
and Cockle Row, it is the grass growing on Llareggub
Hill, dew fall, star fall, the sleep of birds in Milk Wood.

Listen. It is night in the chill, squat chapel, hymning,
in bonnet and brooch and bombazine black, butterfly
choker and bootlace bow, coughing like nannygoats,
sucking mintoes, fortywinking hallelujah; night in the
four-ale, quiet as a domino; in Ocky Milkman's loft like
a mouse with gloves; in Dai Bread's bakery flying like
black flour. It is tonight in Donkey Street, trotting
silent, with seaweed on its hooves, along the cockled
cobbles, past curtained fernpot, text and trinket,
harmonium, holy dresser, watercolours done by hand,
china dog and rosy tin teacaddy. It is night neddying
among the snuggeries of babies.

Look. It is night, dumbly, royally winding through the
Coronation cherry trees; going through the graveyard of
Bethesda with winds gloved and folded, and dew doffed;
tumbling by the Sailors Arms.

Time passes. Listen. Time passes.

Come closer now.

Only you can hear the houses sleeping in the streets in
the slow deep salt and silent black, bandaged night.
Only you can see, in the blinded bedrooms, the corns
and petticoats over the chairs, the jugs and basins, the
glasses of teeth, Thou Shalt Not on the wall, and the
yellowing dickybird-watching pictures of the dead. Only
you can hear and see, behind the eyes of the sleepers,
the movements and countries and mazes and colours
and dismays and rainbows and tunes and wishes and
flight and fall and despairs and big seas of their dreams.

From where you are, you can hear their dreams.

SET PIECES: NOCTURNE

Sarah Wardle

Dug deep in dark despair at dead of night,
depression holds me prisoner from sleep.
That my fond arms lie empty is not right.
I, unrequited, cannot help but weep,
relinquishing the dreams that will not be,
the sweet, flirtatious glances and the kiss,
which I had hoped one day you'd give to me,
the sense of your first touch that I shall miss.
But as I cry, your features all appear
before my eyes. My mind fills with your voice.
I hear you whisper softly in my ear.
My heart beats breathlessly. It has no choice.
Although you are so far and unaware,
it seems you are beside me and you care.

COMPOSED UPON
WESTMINSTER BRIDGE
September 3, 1802

William Wordsworth

Earth has not anything to show more fair:
Dull would he be of soul who could pass by
A sight so touching in its majesty:
This city now doth, like a garment, wear
The beauty of the morning; silent, bare,
Ships, towers, domes, theatres, and temples lie
Open unto the fields, and to the sky;
All bright and glittering in the smokeless air.
Never did sun more beautifully steep
In his first splendour, valley, rock, or hill;
Ne'er saw I, never felt, a calm so deep!
The river glideth at his own sweet will:
Dear God! the very houses seem asleep;
And all that mighty heart is lying still!

ACKNOWLEDGEMENTS

Things by Fleur Adcock is taken from *Poems 1960-2000* (Bloodaxe Books, 2000) and is reprinted by permission of Bloodaxe.

Night Shift by Simon Armitage is taken from *Zoom!* (Bloodaxe Books, 1989) and is reprinted by permission of Bloodaxe.

Dover Beach by Matthew Arnold was first published in 1867.

Night Mail by W.H. Auden is taken from his *Collected Shorter Poems 1927-1957* and is reprinted by permission of Faber and Faber.

Nosferatu by Bob Beagrie is published by permission of the author and is taken from *Huginn & Muninn* (Biscuit Publishing, 2002).

Moon Fox by Peter Bennett appears in *All the Real*, published by Flambard in 1994 and is reprinted by permission of the publisher.

3am Feed by Steven Blyth appeared in *So* (Peterloo, 2001) and appears by permission of the author.

Night Feed by Eavan Boland is published by permission of Carcanet Press and appeared in *Three Irish Poets* (Carcanet, 2003).

Too Late by Alison Brackenbury was previously published in the on-line journal *Snakeskin*, and is printed by permission of the author.

Frost at Midnight by Samuel Taylor Coleridge was first published in 1798.

City Evening by Frances Cornford, from *Travelling Home* (1948) appears by kind permission of the Trustees of the Mrs Frances Crofts Cornford Will Trust.

Silver and **The Listeners** by Walter de la Mare from *The Complete Poems of Walter de la Mare* (1975 reprint) are published by permission of The Literary Trustees of Walter de la Mare and the Society of Authors as their representative.

How We Got Home by Josephine Dickinson appears in *Night Journey*, published by Flambard and is reprinted by permission of the author.

Night Driving by Maura Dooley is from *Sound Barrier: Poems 1982-2002* (Bloodaxe Books, 2002) and is reprinted by permission of the author and publisher.

A Child's Sleep by Carol Ann Duffy is from *Meeting Midnight* (Faber, 1999) and is published by permission of Faber and Faber.

Ode to the Night Shift Freight Worker by Erin E. Elder is published by permission of the author.

Transient Hotel Sky at the Hour of Sleep by Martín Espada was first published in *City of Coughing and Dead Radiators* (W.W. Norton, 1993); **The Bouncer's Confession** was first published in *Imagine the Angels of Bread* (WW Norton, 1996). Both poems are reprinted by permission of the author.

Prayer by Elaine Feinstein is taken from *Daylight* (Carcanet, 1997) and appears by permission of the publisher.

Accounting by Linda France appears in *Storyville* (Bloodaxe, 1997) and is reprinted by permission of the author.

Fire by Wilfred Gibson is from *Collected Poems* and is reprinted by permission of MacMillan Publishers Ltd. © W.W. Gibson, 1929.

The Night City by W.S. Graham is taken from *Selected Poems* (Faber, 1996) and is reprinted by permission of Michael Snow.

Sleeping Bin Bags by Atar Hadari is published here for the first time and is printed by permission of the author.

Night Shift by Karen Jane Glenn first appeared in *North American Review* and on NPR's *All Things Considered*.

Nights at the Mine – I'm on Security by John Harrision was first published in *Shutdown Fortnight* (Mudfog Press, 2007) and appears by permission of the author.

Night by Mark Haworth-Booth was printed in *Wild Track* and is published by courtesy of Trace Editions (www.traceisnotaplace.com).

Night-Watch Man & Muse by Mark Murphy is published by permission of the author and is published here for the first time.

Atlas Moth by Pascale Petit is published by permission of the author. It appears in *The Treekeeper's Tale* (Seren) and was previously published in *Poetry Review* and *Quadrant* (Australia).

Insomniac by Sylvia Plath appears in her *Collected Poems* and is reprinted by permission of Faber and Faber.

Night by Miklós Radnóti is from *Forced March*, translated by George Gömöri and Clive Wilmer (Enitharmon Press, 2003) and appears by permission of the publisher.

Moonrise by Tom Rawling is reprinted from *The Names of the Sea Trout* (Littlewood Arc, 1993) and appears by permission of Arc Publications, © Sue Stater and Jane Rawling.

Constellations by Neil Rollinson appeared in *Spanish Fly*, published by Jonathan Cape. Reprinted by permission of The Random House Group Ltd.

Night Snow by Jane Routh appears by permission of the author.

Sheffield by Night by Peter Sansom appeared in *Poetry: the Nottingham Collection* (Five Leaves, 2005) and is printed by permission of the author.

A Numinous Event by Vernon Scannell appeared in *Behind the Lines* (Shoestring Press) and is printed by permission of the publisher and Joy Scannell.

The Birkdale Nightingale by Jean Sprackland is published by permission of the author and Jonathan Cape and is taken from her collection *Tilt*.

Night Walking with Shadows by Anne Stevenson is from *Poems 1955-2005* (Bloodaxe Books, 2005) and is reprinted by permission of the publisher.

The Bat by Matthew Sweeney first appeared in *The Lame Waltzer* (Alison & Busby, 1985) and is reprinted by permission of the author.

The Fore Shift by Matthew Tate was first published in the *Newcastle Weekly Chronicle* in 1886 and reproduced in A.L. Lloyd (ed) *Come All Ye Bold Miners* (Lawrence and Wishart, 1978).

In Memoriam by Alfred, Lord Tennyson was first published in 1850.

The extract from **Under Milk Wood** by Dylan Thomas (Dent) is published by permission of David Higham Associates Limited.

Set Pieces: Nocturne by Sarah Wardle is taken from *Fields Away* (Bloodaxe Books, 2002) and is reprinted by permission of Bloodaxe.

Composed upon Westminster Bridge by William Wordsworth was written in 1802.

Bewick Swans Arrive at Ouse Washes by Lynne Wycherley appeared in *At the Edge Of Light* (Shoestring Press, 2003).

We have made every effort to trace the copyright holders of all the material included. The publisher would be pleased to hear from any copyright holder who has not been acknowledged so that their details can be added in any subsequent edition.

We would like to thank John Humphrys and Mandy Ross for their help in making this publication possible.